dabble lab

AMAZING MAGIC TRICKS

ABRACADABRA!

TRICKS FOR *ROOKIE* MAGICIANS

4D™

A MAGICAL AUGMENTED
READING
EXPERIENCE

• • • BY NORM BARNHART • • •

CAPSTONE PRESS
a capstone imprint

Dabble Lab is published by
Capstone Press, A Capstone Imprint
1710 Roe Crest Drive
North Mankato, Minnesota 56003
www.mycapstone.com

Library of Congress Cataloging-in-Publication Data
Names: Barnhart, Norm, author.
Title: Abracadabra! : tricks for rookie magicians : 4D a magical augmented reading experience / by Norm Barnhart.
Description: Mankato, Minnesota : Capstone Press, 2018. | Series: Dabble lab. Amazing magic tricks 4D | Includes bibliographical references and index. | Audience: Age 8-12. | Audience: Grade 4 to 6.
Identifiers: LCCN 2017035462 (print) | LCCN 2017039148 (ebook) | ISBN 9781543505733 (eBook PDF) | ISBN 9781543505689 (library binding)
Subjects: LCSH: Magic tricks—Juvenile literature.
Classification: LCC GV1548 (ebook) | LCC GV1548 .B35198 2018 (print) | DDC 793.8—dc23
LC record available at https://lccn.loc.gov/2017035462

• • • • • •

EDITOR:
Aaron J. Sautter

DESIGNER:
Ted Williams

PRODUCTION:
Katy LaVigne

• • • • • •

Image Credits
All photographs and video are done by Capstone Studio

Design Elements
Shutterstock: findracadabra, G.roman, javarman, popular business

Printed and bound in the USA.
010758S18

TABLE OF CONTENTS

......

AMAZING MAGIC!

You don't need to be a master magician to perform magic. With this book, you'll learn simple, fun tricks that will amaze your friends. You can make objects magically appear or disappear right before their eyes! It's easy when you know the secret. Pick up your magic wand and get ready to learn some amazing magic!

THE KEYS TO MAGIC

⭐ **Practice, practice, practice!** Try standing in front of a mirror while practicing with your props. Then you can see what the tricks look like to your audience.

⭐ **Keep it secret!** If you reveal the secrets of a trick, people won't be very impressed. It also ruins the trick for other magicians.

⭐ **Be entertaining!** Tell the audience jokes or stories while you do your tricks. It will keep them coming back for more.

A MAGIC SECRET — PALMING

Magicians often use a method called palming to make things seem to vanish out of thin air. To do it, they secretly hide an object in the palm of their hand. Try practicing palming in front of a mirror so your hand looks natural. Once you learn to palm objects, you'll be able to amaze your friends!

DOWNLOAD THE CAPSTONE 4D APP!

- Ask an adult to search in the Apple App Store or Google Play for "Capstone 4D".
- Click Install (Android) or Get, then Install (Apple).
- Open the app.
- Scan any of the following spreads with this icon:

When you scan a spread, you'll find fun extra stuff to go with this book!
You can also find these things on the web at
www.capstone4D.com using the password **magic.rookie**

MEET THE MAGICIAN! ⭐

Norm Barnhart is a professional comic magician who has entertained audiences for nearly 40 years. In 2007 Norm was named America's Funniest Magician by the Family Entertainers Workshop. Norm's travels have taken him across the United States and to many countries around the world. He also loves to get kids excited about reading. Norm says, **"I love to bring smiles to people of all ages with magic. After reading this book, kids will love performing magic tricks for their friends too."**

THE MAGICAL SAILOR'S KNOT

Magicians need fast hands. In this trick, you'll make a knot instantly appear on a rope. Your friends will be amazed at your incredible hand speed!

WHAT YOU NEED

⭐ A piece of rope about 2 feet (0.6 meters) long

PREPARATION

1. Tie a large knot in one end of the rope as shown.

PERFORMANCE

1. First, show the audience the rope. Hold it with the knot secretly hidden in your hand as shown.

MAGIC TIP

By failing at first, the audience will be more amazed when you make the knot seem to magically appear.

2. Now, hold the other end of the rope between your thumb and first finger. Be sure to keep the knot hidden. Tell the audience that your hands are faster than the eye, and that you can make a knot appear out of thin air.

3. With your free hand, pretend to grab an invisible knot out of the air. Then toss it at the rope.

As you toss the invisible knot, let go of the untied end. Say, "Oops, I missed. I'll try again."

4. Hold the untied end up like before. Pretend to throw the invisible knot again and drop the untied end. Say, "Wow, I missed again." Act a bit disappointed and then try a third time.

The third time it will work. This time let go of the end with the knot. The knot magically appears on the rope!

SEE HOW IT'S DONE

TRICKY TREATS

Everybody loves candy. Wouldn't it be great if you could make candy appear out of nowhere? You can do just that with this quick and easy hanky trick.

PREPARATION

1. Hold the candy between your thumb and fingers as shown. It's best to use wrapped candy so your hand doesn't get sticky.

2. Next, hold the hanky in the fingers of the same hand so the candy is hidden. The audience will think you're only holding the hanky.

1. Wave the hanky in the air and act as if it's empty. Nobody should suspect that you're hiding the candy in that hand. Then place the hanky over the palm of your empty hand as shown.

2. Next, drag the hanky across your open hand. Show the audience that your hand is empty. This step helps people believe that there is nothing there.

3. Now, pull the hanky across your hand again. This time, drop the candy into your open hand. The candy magically appears! Give the candy to someone in the audience to enjoy during the show.

SEE HOW IT'S DONE

FIND THE MAGIC RABBIT

Lots of magicians like pulling rabbits out of their hats. But there's more than one way to find a magic rabbit. In this trick, a magical paper bunny is the star of the show!

PREPARATION

1. Draw a carrot, a bunny, and a hat on the paper as shown. Make sure the bunny is in the middle section. Leave plenty of space between each picture.

PERFORMANCE

1. First, show the audience the paper with the three pictures. Then fold the paper between the pictures and tear it into three pieces along the folds.

MAGIC TIP

Try this trick with some different drawings. You could draw the faces of two boys and a girl, or two dogs and a cat.

2. Next, turn the pictures over. Ask a volunteer to mix the pictures up and cover them with the hanky while your back is turned.

3. When the volunteer is finished, turn back to the table. With a mysterious look on your face say, "I can find the bunny without looking under the hanky." Then reach under the hanky to get the rabbit.

Torn sides

4. Now, pull out the picture of the rabbit and take a bow! The secret to this trick is easy. When you reach under the hanky, simply feel the sides of each piece of paper. Since the rabbit is drawn on the center piece, it is the only paper with two torn sides. It's a simple trick that will keep your friends guessing how it's done!

SEE HOW IT'S DONE

JACK, THE INCREDIBLE CARD

That Jack of Diamonds is one strong card. This super stunt will amaze your friends. They'll watch in wonder as Jack balances a cup on his top edge!

WHAT YOU NEED

- ✪ One Jack of Diamonds card
- ✪ One other card
- ✪ A foam cup
- ✪ Tape
- ✪ Scissors

PREPARATION

1. First, cut the extra card in half lengthwise as shown.

2. Next, tape one half of the cut card to the back of the Jack of Diamonds as shown. This creates a secret flap. When the flap is down, the back of the Jack should look like a normal card.

MAGIC TIP

Always keep the back of the card toward you when the flap is out. Otherwise the secret of the trick will be revealed.

1. Hold up the cup and the Jack card. Show the audience both sides of the card and say, "Jack looks like a normal card, but he's really strong. He can do an amazing balancing act."

2. Now, place the cup on the edge of the card. Secretly pull out the flap to balance the cup as shown.

3. Finally, pull your hand away to show that the Jack card is balancing the cup. Ask the audience to give Jack a round of applause and have him take a bow!

SEE HOW IT'S DONE

13

THE WONDERFUL APPEARING WAND

Every magician needs a magic wand. This trick will astound your audience as your magic wand appears in an impossible way.

WHAT YOU NEED

- A magic wand
- A large box of candy
- Scissors
- A long-sleeved shirt

PREPARATION

1. First, take the candy out of the box and save some for later. Then cut a small hole in the bottom of the box. Make sure the hole is a little larger than your magic wand.

2. Next, slide the wand up your sleeve as shown. When you're ready to do the trick, you'll simply slide the wand through the hole in the box. Put a few pieces of the candy you saved back in the box.

1

Secret
hole

1. First, go to your magic trunk to get the candy box. While your hands are hidden, slide the end of the wand through the secret hole in the candy box. Then show the candy box to your audience. Say, "I like this candy. One in every ten thousand boxes has a special gift!" Be sure to keep the secret hole hidden in your hand.

2. Now, start eating some of the candy from the box. As you eat, pretend that you find something inside. Act surprised, and then reach in and start pulling out the magic wand.

2

3. Finally, pull the wand out of the box and show it to the audience. Say, "Wow, this is my lucky day!" Now you have a magic wand to help you perform the rest of your show!

3

SEE HOW IT'S DONE

15

INVISIBLE MAGIC GLUE

Your friends will wonder how your wand sticks to your hand with this mysterious trick. They'll be amazed when the wand falls off with a snap of their fingers!

WHAT YOU NEED

⭐ A magic wand
⭐ A small empty bottle

PEFORMANCE

1. Any small bottle will work for this trick. Start by telling your audience that the bottle holds invisible magic glue.

Next, hold your wand in one hand and pretend to pour the glue all over the wand and your hand.

2. Close your hand around the wand and put the bottle back in your magic trunk.

Now, grip your wrist with your other hand. Slide your finger up to hold the wand as shown, hiding it behind your open hand. Keep your wand and finger facing away from the audience. If your friends see your finger, the trick will be ruined!

3. Next, slowly open your hand to show that the wand is stuck in place. Say, "This invisible glue is some really sticky stuff!"

4. When you want the glue to disappear, just ask a friend to snap his or her fingers. At that moment, let the wand go by moving your finger. The wand is no longer stuck to your hand!

MAGIC TIP   Try using your acting skills to add humor to this trick. Pretend that the wand won't come off, no matter how hard you shake your hand!

SEE HOW IT'S DONE

THE AMAZING APPEARING BALL

"Where did that ball come from?" That's what your friends will say when you make this ball magically appear from an empty cup!

WHAT YOU NEED

* A ping-pong ball
* A foam cup
* A magic wand

PREPARATION

1. First, poke a hole in the foam cup so your finger can slip into it.

Now, place the ball in the cup and use your third finger to hold it in place as shown.

MAGIC TIP Add some fun to this trick by drawing a face on the ball and giving it a fun name. Pretend that it likes to play hide-and-seek!

1. First, tip over the cup to show that it's empty. Then tell the audience, "Things aren't always how they appear. This cup might look empty, but it's not." Be sure not to let anyone see the ball or your finger inside the cup!

2. Now, hold the cup up high and wave your magic wand over it. While you do this, you can say a few made-up magic words.

3. Finally, tip over the cup and let the ball fall into your open hand. The ball magically appears!

Show the audience the ball and toss it to someone. While they're looking at the ball, toss the special cup into your magic trunk. Nobody will ever know the secret!

SEE HOW IT'S DONE

THE FANTASTIC FLOWER

Flowers grow quickly in the spring. But with this trick, you can make a flower appear instantly with special magic seeds. Your friends will be really impressed!

WHAT YOU NEED

⭐ A small flower pot
⭐ A fake flower
⭐ An empty seed packet
⭐ A magic wand

PREPARATION

1. Place the flower in the flower pot. Then put the pot in your magic trunk.

PERFORMANCE

1. When you're ready to do this trick, hide the flower by holding it against the side of the pot as shown.

2. Hold up the pot to show the audience that it's empty. Be sure to keep the flower hidden under your hand. Put down the flowerpot and release the hidden flower inside. Then take out the empty seed packet.

Hidden flower

3. Tell the audience about your magic flower seeds. Say, "These are the world's fastest growing flowers." Pretend to sprinkle some invisible seeds from the seed packet into the flower pot.

Next, pretend to add some magical sunshine and rain to help the flower grow.

Finally, wave your magic wand over the pot and say a few magic words.

4. Now, reach in and pull out the pretty flower that has magically grown inside! You can give the flower to your mom or a friend as a gift.

SEE HOW IT'S DONE

21

THE MYSTERIOUS CAR TRICK

You can use the power of your mind to find a shiny, cool car hidden in a paper bag. Your incredible mental powers will baffle people with this trick!

WHAT YOU NEED

- Three small paper bags
- One shiny toy car
- Two dull toy cars
- A pencil

PREPARATION

1. Place a small, secret pencil mark in the bottom corner of one bag as shown. Don't make the mark too dark, or someone might see it and learn how this trick works.

Secret mark

PERFORMANCE

1. First, show the three cars to the audience. Place the shiny cool car in the marked bag. Place the dull cars in the other bags. Then fold over the tops of all three bags. Keep the secret mark facing you so nobody sees it.

MAGIC TIP

Try acting like you don't know which bag is correct at first. Ask the volunteer to help by mixing up the bags even more. The audience will be astonished when you find the cool car!

2. Tell the audience about your amazing mental powers. Say, "I can use my mind to find the cool car even if the bags are mixed up." Then turn around and ask a volunteer from the audience to mix up the bags.

3. Now, turn back to the table and pretend to use your mind powers to find the cool car. Hold up each bag and look at it closely. Pretend to concentrate hard on what's inside. While doing this, you will really be looking for the bag with the secret mark.

4. When you find the marked bag say, "This is it! I've found the cool car." Reach in and pull out the cool car. Take a bow as the audience applauds your amazing mental powers!

SEE HOW IT'S DONE

ZARCON, THE INVISIBLE HERO

The alien hero Zarcon has worked hard to bring criminals to justice. Now it's time for him to go home. With a wave of your magic wand, he disappears and travels back to his own planet.

WHAT YOU NEED

⭐ A colorful handkerchief ⭐ A secret helper
⭐ A small action figure ⭐ A magic wand

PERFORMANCE

1. Show Zarcon to the audience and tell them he wants to return to his home planet. Tell them that you're going to help him with a bit of magic. When you're ready for the trick, hold the toy in your hand as shown.

2. Next, place the hanky over your hand to hide Zarcon as shown.

MAGIC TIP

Be sure to practice this trick with your secret helper ahead of time. Make it look smooth and natural, and the audience won't suspect a thing.

24

3. Now, ask two volunteers to feel under the hanky to make sure Zarcon hasn't disappeared yet.

4. The second person will really be your secret helper. Your helper will secretly take Zarcon from your hand as shown, and then hide the toy in his or her pocket. Ask your secret helper, "Is Zarcon still there?" He or she should say, "Yes."

5. After your helper takes Zarcon, wave your magic wand over the hanky. Finally, remove the hanky and show the audience that Zarcon has disappeared!

SEE HOW IT'S DONE

FAST RABBIT AND THE ACE

People love card tricks. They love to watch cards magically switch locations or change colors. In this trick, your magic rabbit loves the Ace of Diamonds so much he can't resist stealing it!

PREPARATION

1. First, separate the four Aces from the deck of cards. Place the Ace of Diamonds on top of the deck of cards. Then set the other three Aces on top of the Ace of Diamonds.

MAGIC TIP   If you don't have a bunny, you can use any other small stuffed toy for this trick.

1. Introduce your stuffed bunny to the audience. Tell them he really loves the Ace of Diamonds. Say that he sometimes steals it so fast that you can't even see him move!

Take the three Aces from the top of the deck and set them aside. Be sure to leave the Ace of Diamonds on top of the deck. Then place the bunny on top of the deck.

2. Arrange the other three aces with the Ace of Hearts behind the black Aces as shown. Hold the cards close together so the Ace of Hearts looks like the Ace of Diamonds as seen in the second picture above. Then ask a volunteer to help with this trick. Show the volunteer the Aces. Ask if he or she sees the Ace of Diamonds. The volunteer should say, "Yes."

27

3. Next, lay the Aces face down one by one on the table. Make sure the volunteer doesn't see the front of the cards. Ask the volunteer to guess which card is the Ace of Diamonds. He or she will probably pick the middle card.

4. Flip the card over to show that it is really the Ace of Hearts. Your volunteer will probably be surprised! Ask the volunteer to try picking a different card.

5. Flip over the next chosen card. It won't be the Ace of Diamonds either. Do this again with the third card so all three aces are face up.

6. It's time to show where the Ace of Diamonds went. Say, "Look at that — the Ace of Diamonds is gone! I bet my magic bunny ran over and stole it so fast that we couldn't see it."

Lift the bunny off the deck of cards. Pick up the top card and show that he's been sitting on the Ace of Diamonds! Thank your volunteer and have the bunny take a bow.

SEE HOW IT'S DONE

29

GLOSSARY

astound (uh-STOUND)—to amaze or astonish

audience (AW-dee-uhns)—people who watch or listen to a play, movie, or show

balance (BA-luhnts)—to keep steady and not fall over

concentrate (KAHN-suhn-trayt)—to focus your thoughts and attention on something

humor (HYOO-mor)—the funny or amusing quality of something

justice (JUHSS-tiss)—when punishment is given for breaking the law

mental power (MEN-tuhl POW-ur)—the ability to do something with the mind, such as finding hidden objects or reading others' thoughts

palming (PALM-ing)—to hide something in the palm of your hand

prop (PROP)—an item used by an actor or performer during a show

trunk (TRUHNGK)—a large case or box used for storage or for carrying items

volunteer (vol-uhn-TIHR)—someone who offers to help perform a task during a show

READ MORE

Barnhart, Norm. *Marvelous Money Tricks.* Magic Manuals. North Mankato, Minn.: Capstone Press, 2014.

Kelly, Kristen and Ken Kelly. *Abracadabra! Fun Magic Tricks for Kids.* New York: Skyhorse Publishing, 2016.

Turnbull, Stephanie. *Easy Card Tricks.* Beginner Magic. Mankato, Minn.: Smart Apple Media, 2014.

· · · · · ·

INTERNET SITES

Use FactHound to find Internet sites related to this book.

Visit www.facthound.com

Just type in 9781543505689 and go.

 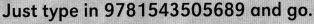

Super-cool stuff! Check out projects, games and lots more at www.capstonekids.com

INDEX